Inflation

What It Is and How It Works

Inflation

What It Is and How It Works

Lisa A. Crayton and Joyce Hart

**Enslow Publishing**
101 W. 23rd Street
Suite 240
New York, NY 10011
USA
enslow.com

Published in 2016 by Enslow Publishing, LLC.
101 W. 23rd Street, Suite 240, New York, NY 10011

Library of Congress Cataloging-in-Publication Data

Crayton, Lisa A.
 Inflation : what it is and how it works / Lisa A. Crayton and Joyce Hart.
  pages cm. — (Economics in the 21st century)
 Includes bibliographical references and index.
 ISBN 978-0-7660-7248-0
1. Inflation (Finance)—Juvenile literature. I. Hart, Joyce, 1954- II. Title.
 HG229.C73 2016
 332.4'1—dc23
                    2015029188

Printed in the United States of America

To Our Readers: We have done our best to make sure all website addresses in this book were active and appropriate when we went to press. However, the author and the publisher have no control over and assume no liability for the material available on those websites or on any websites they may link to. Any comments or suggestions can be sent by e-mail to customerservice@enslow.com.

Portions of this text were originally written by Joyce Hart.

Contents

CHAPTER 1
What Is Inflation?

W hat do beach balls, balloons and moon bounces have in common? If your answer is "they are all fun play items," you are partially correct. One other similarity: They all go through a process called inflation. Generally, inflation is any expansion or increase. When you blow air into a balloon, for example, it expands until reaching its maximum capacity—or pops. This basic understanding of inflation also encompasses how bicycle and car tires are filled to restore air, balance, and functionality.

For purposes of this book, inflation also is defined as an expansion or increase. In economics terms it specifically defines a rise in the cost of living, especially continual rises in the general price of goods and services. When the economy experiences inflation, we feel it in nearly every area of life as prices soar higher than the year before. Higher food prices mean less money for snacks and other non-essential food items because prices are simply too high. When prices of school uniforms, athletic shoes, and other gear nudge upward, it's more difficult to buy the same number of items with the same back-to-school shopping budget. Fuel costs make it more costly to heat homes and businesses, and for airlines to fly planes.

Another affected area: transportation. A hike in gas prices affects commuters and school systems. Commuters make decisions whether to decrease the number of days they drive in and use public transportation instead.

Meanwhile, affected school systems must use innovative, affordable ways of financing school transportation programs. One method is to use fewer buses by condensing the number of routes, resulting in more crowded school buses! Clearly, inflation affects us in many ways—big and small. This is why it is important to know what inflation is and how it works.

Some Good News

Under some conditions, inflation is good. Inflation helps to boost profits for the people who make goods. This, in turn, helps the economy because those profits might be reinvested. For example, if a business makes extra money, the owners might share those profits with their employees. So one day, your mom or dad might come home and say, "I got a raise." This means he or she is now making more money. To celebrate, your parents might go out and buy a new car or invest in a new computer and a new library of computer games. When your parents—and other people in your community and around the country—purchase new items, the stores from which they bought those goods also celebrate. They are making more money, too.

If inflation is not controlled, however, the economy can suffer. If prices on goods continue to rise, and your parents' salaries do not increase, then new cars, new computers, and even food can cost more money than some people can afford. Their income, or earnings, is not keeping up with inflation.

Many economists believe that a healthy rate of inflation is around a 3 percent increase each year. This means that prices rise from one year to the next at a rate of 3 percent, or three pennies per dollar spent. So, if it costs you $10 to rent a Wii game this year, next year that same game would cost $10.30 to rent. Now imagine buying an Xbox One game at today's steep prices, and paying 3 percent more next year! A 3 percent rise in inflation

Sometimes inflation is good. A company that makes more money than expected might give employees a raise. Those employees might spend their raises in the community, so those businesses make money, too.

is not difficult to handle for most people who are employed (have a job). Most likely, many of them receive raises every year, which helps to offset a 3 percent inflation hike on the cost of goods. Affordability diminishes when the item is already pricey, like the Xbox One game, and its price climbs higher the following year.

There are ways of controlling inflation, which will be discussed later in this resource. But to give you an example of how this might work in your own life, let's look at a hypothetical (make-believe) situation.

Suppose you had a friend named Ian whose family owned a lemon orchard. In the summer, Ian set up a lemonade stand and sold some of the best lemonade you ever tasted. You and all your neighbors looked forward to seeing Ian at his stand, and you all bought tall glasses of lemonade faster than Ian could make it. So this year, Ian decided to raise the price from $1 to $2 per glass. The first time you went to his stand, you were shocked by this inflated price. However, you were very thirsty, so you paid the extra dollar.

But as the summer went along, you and your neighbors started complaining about the extra money that Ian was charging. No one could afford the new high price, so everyone stopped going to Ian's stand. Ian sat there all day waiting for people to come by, but no one did. All the lemonade he had made went bad, and he had to throw it away. This went on for a week. Eventually, Ian figured it out. He finally realized that he had to lower his price to lure his customers back to his stand. Ian put up new signs, advertising that the price had been cut in half. He was once again selling lemonade at a price of $1 per glass. You and your neighbors, who were eager to drink the greatest lemonade in the world, almost ran back to Ian's stand. Soon, Ian's business was thriving again.

Inflation at a rate of about 3 percent is generally considered a good thing.
It's not a big deal to pay an extra 3 percent on smaller items like video games.

Economies of large countries like the United States are not quite as simple as Ian's lemonade stand. However, some of the same economic principles are used by the federal government to help control various kinds of inflation. The government wants to make sure that inflation does not get out of control. There is a constant monitoring of the economy to make sure that goods (like food and gasoline) and services (like hospitals and public transportation) are affordable. In other words, the economy of a country works best when people are making enough money to buy the things they need and want. Therefore, the government makes adjustments so that businesses can remain successful, while at the same time making it possible for people to afford to buy their goods.

A Closer Look at Inflation

Inflation is more than just an increase in the cost of goods and services. For economists to declare that a country's economy is indeed in a state of inflation, the cost of food, gasoline, and other important goods that people need have to not only rise significantly, but this rise also has to last over a relatively long period of time. What this means is that the price of a movie ticket might increase from $10 to $12 over a period of two years, but this does not necessarily mean that the economy is suffering the effects of inflation. This might just mean that the owner of the movie theater wants to make a bigger profit. A profit is the extra money a business owner makes after all expenses have been paid. The theater owner might be betting that enough people want to see movies badly enough that they will pay the extra money for tickets. The price he charges rises even though his operating expenses have not risen at the same rate. So, his price increase is a profit-driven choice he makes, rather than something he has to do to stay in business.

Increased movie ticket prices can mean the theater wants to make a profit. Inflation might be the cause, however, if the owner's decision is because she needs to cover increasing expenses.

If the US government were to print more paper money without having
the funds to back it up, then all the paper bills would be worth less.

If, however, the owner has raised ticket prices to cover his own increasing
costs of doing business, and ticket prices remain high for a long period of
time, this would be a symptom of inflation.

Economists identify inflation in different ways. One of the ways is to
calculate how much purchasing (or buying) power consumers are enjoying.
For example, economists might measure if $50 buys as much food today as
it did two years ago. If their research finds that the answer to this question
is that $50 buys just as much today as it did two years ago, then there is no
inflation in the food market. But they might not end their research there.
They might ask other questions. Does $50 buy as much gasoline as it did
two years ago? They might examine the price of clothing or how much it
costs to visit a doctor. If they find significant price increases in any of the

major goods or services, then they analyze the results further. They will want to know how big the price increases are and how these increases are affecting families. Even if food prices are not inflated, the inflated costs of other goods and services might be causing families serious financial difficulties.

Another term that economists use in reference to inflation is "hyperinflation." In 2008, Zimbabwe was suffering an inflation rate of more than 2 million percent. Economists call this hyperinflation because Zimbabwe's inflation was rising unusually fast. Hyperinflation most often occurs when a government prints too much money, which is one of the things that was happening in Zimbabwe. The more money that a government prints, the less value that money has. The less value that money has, the higher the prices rise because greater amounts of the less valuable currency are needed to buy things.

Understanding "Worth"

As a practical example of how devalued currency works, imagine that you own one of the rarest cards in the whole Pokémon series. What would you be willing to trade for this rare card? Now, imagine that everyone just learned that this rare card you own has been duplicated by the company that makes Pokémon cards. Now, instead of there being just 100 cards in the world, there are 100 million of them. Because the company has made so many copies of this once-rare card, the value of your Pokémon card has just been devalued. It is now far less valuable than it was when it was rare. In comparison with how many cards you once might have requested in exchange for trading your rare card, the value of your card has now been greatly diminished. You will receive many fewer cards in a trade for it.

This same procedure works with a nation's currency. Paper money is valued because of standards that a country sets for those paper bills. For instance, let's pretend that there is a country that has a paper currency called the "dangle." That country prints 10,000 dangle bills made of paper. The paper is not worth anything by itself. However, if the country guarantees that one dangle stands for one ounce of silver and that same country promises that it has 10,000 ounces of silver available in its bank, then a paper dangle is worth something. One dangle is worth one ounce of silver.

But one year later, let's say that the government wants to increase its currency (wants to make more money), so it prints 10,000 more dangles. Unfortunately, that same country does not have 10,000 more ounces of silver to back up this new printing of paper dangles. So, the 10,000 paper dangles plus the original 10,000 dangles are not worth an ounce of silver each. They are now worth only half an ounce of silver. Although a citizen of this country might have been able to buy a bike for one dangle last year, that same bike now costs two dangles. Imagine how much less a dangle would be worth if the government had printed one million more dangles without increasing the amount of silver in its bank to back up the currency. This is one of the causes of hyperinflation, and it is exactly what has happened in Zimbabwe.

Inflation Origins

Just as inflation might be identified in a variety of ways, there are also different causes of inflation, including an increase in the demand for a product and an increase in production costs.

The Pull of Demand

Demand-pull inflation occurs when a lot of people in households, the government, businesses, or foreign countries want to buy something, but there are not enough goods or services available. Let's go back to Ian's

If the supply of lemons is limited but people are still willing
to buy them, the demand may increase the price.

lemonade stand to understand how an increase in demand can result in higher prices.

It was a hard winter for Ian's parents' orchard. A late winter frost killed many of the lemons. So in the spring and summer months, when Ian's neighbors came to Ian's lemonade stand, they found only one pitcher of lemonade. Ian sold ten glasses of lemonade, but there were fifteen people who stood in line. This means that five people went home without tasting the lemonade.

Those five people who did not get the lemonade the first day rushed to Ian's stand very early the next morning. They wanted to make sure they would be first in line for the new batch of juice that Ian was making. The news had gotten out that there was only a small supply of lemonade this year. So another twenty people came running to Ian's stand, too, hoping to get a taste of the lemonade before the supply completely ran out. Again, Ian had only enough lemonade for ten people. So, fifteen people went home without tasting the sweet drink.

On the third day, even more people showed up at the stand. There was some pushing and shoving going on for the first ten places in line. Ian realized that his lemonade was in high demand. People really wanted his lemonade. He wondered what would happen if he changed his price from $1 per glass to $2 per glass. He soon found out. Some people left because they refused to pay the 100 percent inflated price. But ten people paid the doubled price, and Ian made a big profit.

In this example, the demand for the lemonade pulled the price up, causing the inflation. This type of inflation often happens in business, especially when a new product, such as the long-awaited Nintendo electronic game player Wii, first come out on the market. So many people wanted to buy the Wii that Nintendo could not keep up with the demand. So, the price of the Wii remained high. Once most of the orders for the Wii were met and not as many people wanted to buy it, then the company lowered the price to encourage more reluctant or less enthusiastic consumers to buy it.

Pushed by Costs

Cost-push inflation occurs when a company's costs go up. This might be caused by a variety of incidents, such as having to pay higher taxes or higher salaries or experiencing an increase in the cost of supplies that are needed to make the company's products.

For example, let's say that Ian had three major new costs before he opened his lemonade stand this year. First, the wood in Ian's old stand rotted, and he had to build a new stand. The wood was expensive, costing him $30. Second, last year he received a notice from the city, stating that he would have to buy a permit that gave him the city's permission to sell lemonade on the street. The permit cost Ian $15. Third, last summer some people had complained that the lemonade was too warm. Ian's customers asked if they could have some ice in the lemonade. So, Ian bought a cooler to keep the ice in. This cost him another $15. Ian had extra costs this year that amounted to $60.

To make as much money as he did last year, Ian calculated that he would have to raise the cost of each glass of lemonade to $1.50. The extra costs that Ian had to pay for the new supplies and the permit "pushed up" the need for the inflated price of lemonade.

Cost-push inflation often occurs in a business when its workers' salaries, production and supply costs, and other expenses are higher than the amount of money that the owner can make in selling the business's goods or services.

Gold Standard No Longer

Although the US currency used to be backed by gold or silver, this is no longer true. Today, the US currency's worth is based on the potential wealth of the country. In other words, the worth of US currency depends on the money that American citizens and businesses will make in the future and on the taxes on that income and wealth that they will pay to the government. The US currency, therefore, has worth not in and of itself (it's only paper), but rather because it symbolizes wealth and can be used to trade for goods and services. The US dollar, in other words, has become a medium of exchange.

US money can be used to exchange goods and services, but you can no longer go to a bank with a $10 bill and ask for the $10 worth of gold that once backed that bill.

A good example of this is the airline business. Airlines sell the service of transportation. Pilots, who fly the planes, need to be well trained and experienced. To attract the best pilots, an airline has to pay them a good salary. In 2008, when the price of gasoline doubled, the airline business had to pay a lot more money to buy supplies (expensive gasoline to fuel the planes). To pay for these fuel and personnel costs, the airlines raised the cost of airline tickets. They also added extra charges for checking in suitcases, for using pillows and blankets, and for drinking beverages (which used to be free). These extra charges helped the airlines cover their costs. The higher prices for the airline tickets were the result of cost-push inflation.

CHAPTER 2
The Currency Connection

I nflation is not a new phenomenon. It's been around throughout history from the early days of paying for goods and services. Price swings occurred based on supply and demand. Prices increased when demand for items outpaced the supply. That is very similar to what happens today. When there are more people wanting smartphones than there are smartphones available, then the price nudges upward—or skyrockets. Now you know why iPhones cost so much!

Again, historically, inflation only kicked in once payment came into the picture. Before there was a form of money, people used to barter for goods and services. This means that people would make deals with one another and then swap one set of goods or services for another. For example, a goat herder might barter with a farmer by offering goats' milk or goats' cheese in exchange for the farmer's corn or wheat. A tailor might offer to make a new suit of clothes for a livestock owner in exchange for a horse.

If there were a lot of farmers in one village who raised chickens that produced more eggs than the villagers could eat, then the value of the eggs might be fairly low. But if there was just one cobbler in the village, he could demand a lot of goods in exchange for a new pair of shoes that he knew how to make. If the value (the worth) of a product is low, so too is its price.

At one time people bartered for their goods and services.
Even after there was a form of money, people sometimes continued
to exchange eggs for dental work, for example.

If something is highly valued, it costs more. The price of something reflects what it is worth, or how highly it is valued.

As time went by and the populations of towns began to grow, pulling a horse all over town or chasing a herd of sheep through the city streets to use as barter became more difficult and inconvenient. So, bartering was not always the best, most efficient way to purchase goods or services. This is when money came into use. But money did not always take the form of coins and paper bills as it does today. In fact, one kind of early money took the form of seashells.

Early Forms of Money

In many ancient cultures, such as in Africa, China, India, and North America before the arrival of Europeans, shells were prized possessions. Shells were used just as people use money today. The shells were different from one culture to another, but they all worked in the same way. Everything that a person might need could be exchanged for a certain number of shells. It wasn't until later, sometime around 3000 BCE, that gold was first used as money. At first, gold nuggets were used. The nuggets had to be weighed during each transaction to guarantee their worth. The more the nugget weighed, the more it was worth. Then, over time, instead of using gold nuggets of random weights, the gold was melted into the form of bars that had a uniform weight. Using gold bars as a form of money was more convenient than pulling a wagon of chickens into town, but gold bars were heavy and still not as portable as our modern forms of money.

Many years later, silver was added as a prized currency. Sometimes gold and silver were made in the form of rings that could be worn on a person's fingers or carried on leather strings. People used the gold and silver rings like we use coins and paper money today.

Shells were once a valuable possession and exchanged
the same way we exchange money today.

During the seventh century BCE, the gold and silver that were used as money were made into coins. The first coins were made in Asia Minor (in the area of modern-day Turkey). About this same time, China also developed metal coins. But the coins were not all made of gold and silver. Other metals, such as bronze, copper, and tin, were also used by ancient cultures. For a while, China even used leather coins.

Coins were also used by the Greeks and the Romans, who mixed cheaper metals in with their gold and silver coins when they needed more money. The less gold and silver in the coins, the less value the coins had. Mixing in cheaper metals to be able to make more coins is the same as today's practice of printing more money without having any additional value to back the new bills. Just like in modern economies, the Greeks and the Romans suffered from inflation when they devalued the coins in this way. As the coins lost value (because they were no longer made of pure gold or silver), more coins were needed to purchase goods and services. That was when inflation set in.

How Paper Money Developed

The Chinese were the first to issue paper money, around 806 CE. They created paper bills because they were running low on copper, the main metal they used for their coins. Their paper bills were based on real worth and were backed by reserves of precious metals in banks. As in other countries, however, when the Chinese people needed more money, they just printed more paper bills and no longer backed the bills with the same amount of real wealth (such as gold). The paper money began to lose its worth. As in so many instances in which countries increased their money supply without maintaining its worth, inflation in China soared.

This paper and coin currency from the state of New Jersey
around 1750 was used by a soldier.

The American colonies created their own form of money. When it came time to go up against Great Britain during the Revolutionary War (1775–1783), the Continental Congress (the governing body of the original thirteen colonies/states before and during the war) produced paper money called Continentals. At first, the Congress promised that the Continentals would be backed by silver. However, as the war dragged on, the army's expenses grew, and the Congress printed Continentals far beyond the amount of silver they had to back them. By the end of the war, the paper money was almost worthless. This flooding of the economy with lots of money that had little or no real worth caused severe inflation.

Although paper money was used in Europe and in the North American colonies in earlier centuries, it wasn't until 1816 that a gold standard was set for the paper bills. The government in England was the first to set gold as the standard value backing paper money. It did this to stop the inflation that had arisen as a result of banks printing paper money and randomly setting its value, rather than backing the value on actual gold or silver. Most early paper money was more like a promise from the bank that the bills could be exchanged for a certain amount of precious metal. But the banks offered no guarantee that this would actually happen before the gold standard was made the rule.

With the gold standard established in England, each banknote (the paper money) had a specific value in gold. In 1900, the United States passed the Gold Standard Act, which meant that paper money in America would also be backed by gold.

Today, the gold standard no longer exists in either Europe or the United States. Instead, the US dollar is based on the potential wealth of the country

Picture Perfect?

The Treasury Department announced in 2013 that it will redesign the $10 bill around a theme of democracy. It will include new security features and a portrait of someone other than that of Alexander Hamilton, our country's first Secretary of the US Treasury. The announcement sparked mixed reviews. Some people felt the bills should remain as is. Others felt a woman's portrait should be included. Others felt that perhaps there should be two portraits, with Hamilton remaining on the bill in some form. The department invited consumer feedback through social media and the hashtag #TheNew10. In the end, it was decided that a woman (whose name had not been revealed by October 2015) will be featured on the $10 bill's face, beginning in 2020. It did not say whether Hamilton's portrait also will remain. Time will tell.

and the performance of the US economy relative to other countries. American citizens and businesses must pay taxes, for instance, and those taxes become the basis of some of the country's potential wealth. So, as long as the US economy is doing well, the US dollar is considered strong. But when the economy is not doing well—when the country's potential to generate wealth decreases—the US dollar loses its strength. In general, the dollar is worth less during economic downturns than it is during boom times. Because all currencies around the world are not based on the same gold standard, and some are not based on any gold standard at all, the worth of a country's currency constantly rises and falls, depending on how well the country's economy is doing.

Wartime Effects on Inflation

One of the first serious occurrences of inflation in the United States was the result of the Revolutionary War. As stated before, the Continental Congress, instead of raising taxes to pay for the war, authorized multiple increases in the amount of paper money to be printed to finance the war. But the Congress did not back the increased amount of currency with additional amounts of real worth (such as gold or silver). As a result, there was inflation. Inflation often occurs when a country is waging war. The country prints a lot of extra money to pay its bills and to buy military equipment and supplies.

By the end of the war, everyone knew that the money was not backed by real wealth, so the currency became worthless. This also happened during the Civil War, when the Southern states printed their own Confederate money. At the war's end, when the Confederacy no longer existed, the Confederate money had no worth at all.

When the Continental Congress needed to pay for cannons, ammunition, and other wartime necessities for the Revolutionary War, it printed more money without raising taxes, which resulted in inflation.

Wartime inflation is not always because of the government printing more dollar bills than it has actual wealth in the form of silver and gold reserves. Sometimes a government borrows money from another country. When the war is over, that government has to pay back the money it borrowed plus extra money for the interest charged on the loan. When someone loans money, they usually charge the person who is borrowing the money interest.

Interest is a percentage of the money that is borrowed. So, if you borrowed $10 from a bank, the bank might charge you 10 percent interest. This means that you would have to pay back the $10 you borrowed plus the interest, which would be an additional dollar. You would owe the bank $11, even though you borrowed only $10.

Now, imagine if a country borrowed several million dollars. Or, what if a country borrowed billions of dollars? Ten percent interest on just $1 million would be $100,000. What this means is that by the end of a war, a government might owe a bank or another country so much money that it has trouble paying it off. The government might then have to raise taxes on things like gasoline and cigarettes to collect more money to pay back the loan. Higher taxes, in turn, mean that goods and services now cost more money. And that means inflation.

Inflation hit the US economy especially hard during such conflicts as the Civil War, World Wars I and II, the Korean War, and the Vietnam War. During World War II, the price of goods rose at a 7 percent rate of inflation. During World War I, at times, prices rose more than 200 percent.

After World War II, with a few exceptions, inflation in the US economy was kept fairly low. The inflation rate for most of the postwar years to the mid-2000s averaged about 3 percent. Many economists believe that

Cost of Living Comparison
1950s to 2000s

	1950s	1980s	2008	2013
Movie ticket	$0.50	$3.50	$8	$8.13
Loaf of bread	$0.16	$0.51	$2.50	$1.98
Postage stamp	$0.03	$0.20	$0.42	$0.49
Average house	$16,000	$100,000	$250,000	$289,500
Average car	$1,800	$6,000	$20,000	$31,252
Average gallon of gas	$0.20	$1	$4	$3.80
Average salary	$3,000	$16,000	$50,000	$52,250
Average annual tuition at a four-year private college	$1,000	$5,000	$15,000	$30,131

an inflation rate around 3 percent is good for the economy. A 3 percent inflation rate provides healthy profits for businesses, while allowing most people salary increases that can keep up with a moderately rising cost of living. There were higher peaks of inflation, however, such as during the Korean War in the 1950s, when inflation was at 5.9 percent. Also, while America was becoming mired in the Vietnam War during the 1960s and early 1970s, prices in the United States rose at a 5.7 percent rate.

The Fuel Factor

During the 1970s, American citizens saw inflation rates rise even more significantly. In some years of the decade, inflation rose as high as 13 percent. Some of this high inflation was due to the ongoing Vietnam War. Another reason for the high inflation of the 1970s, however, was caused by very high oil prices. The oil-producing nations of the Middle East cut back on the production of oil. This created a high demand for an increasingly limited supply of oil. Americans were soon spending hours in long lines that stretched for blocks at gas stations, waiting to fill their gas tanks. Many gas stations ran out of gas before everyone could fill their tanks. So, people would drive to another gas station or come back to the same station the next day. Eventually, people were assigned days they could show up at a gas station.

This scarcity (lack of supply) created high demand for gasoline, so fuel prices kept rising and quickly became inflated. The gas station owners were forced to pay more money to the companies that produced and supplied the gasoline. Then, to make up for the extra money they were paying to fuel producers and suppliers, the gas station owners charged more for the gas that people pumped into their cars.

In 2008, the price of gasoline also rose sharply. The inflation rate for fuel was much higher than the increase in people's salaries. While in the years prior to 2008 people might have paid $30 to fill up their gas tank, they were now paying $60 or more. When the price of gasoline goes up, so too does the price of food. Farmers, who produce the food, use gasoline to run their tractors and other farm machinery. They also use gasoline to haul their crops to the market.

Farmers pass these extra costs onto the stores that buy their produce and the food processors who use their grain, produce, and meat. And the stores and food processors pass the extra costs onto consumers who buy the food for their families. In times of higher fuel prices, therefore, families are not only spending more money to fill up their cars with gasoline and heat their homes with oil or natural gas, but they are also spending more money on food.

High oil prices also affect businesses. The goods that a business purchases are sometimes transported to its store by large commercial barges that bring the goods across the ocean. Freight trains with diesel engines transport a large percentage of goods, too. Some goods are brought in by air. Then, trucks are used to bring the goods from the airports and the docks. Everyone along the way pays the high cost of fuel. Everyone passes these costs on. So, the store pays more for the goods and passes the extra costs onto the consumer. This means that when you go to the store, you pay more for clothing, games, books, and school supplies.

CHAPTER 3

How Inflation Is Measured

T
o understand inflation it's useful to know what entity is responsible for measuring inflation and how is it measured. The US Department of Labor is the federal government agency responsible for measuring inflation. It attempts to provide a true picture of what is happening around the country regarding inflation, but the task is not easy. Remember, inflation is a continual rise in prices from year to year. As you know if you've visited other cities, prices are not always equal. Products cost more in some cities than they do in others. Another reason measuring inflation is difficult is because the government focuses solely on the cost of living as it relates to people living in cities and urban environments. For these reasons the process of measuring inflation is not perfect—and likely never will be! Despite this, the Department of Labor provides reliable data that helps us understand what is happening in the economy.

How Is Inflation Measured?

The Department of Labor collects the information and then produces what is called the consumer price index (CPI). There are other, similar collections of economic information, but the CPI is the index that is used the most often. The CPI is used to gauge the average change, over time, of what people are spending on goods and services. The department does this by selecting specific goods and services that are routinely bought by consumers. The people who are chosen for the survey are asked to list the goods and services that they buy and how much they pay for them.

A Basket of Goods and Services

The Department of Labor collects information about the buying patterns of people who live in metropolitan (city) areas. They send surveys to urban consumers and urban wage earners. This group, according to the Department of Labor, represents about 87 percent of the entire population of the United States. The department also sends surveys to people who are unemployed, people who are self-employed (people who run their own businesses), and people who are retired. People who live in rural areas of the country, such as farming families, and people who are in the military are not included in the surveys.

It is from this information that the Department of Labor creates what it calls a market basket. This market basket is not a real basket. It is a representation of the most popular items—almost 80,000 goods and services—that people in the United States pay for each year.

To create the market basket, the Department of Labor asks about 7,000 families from around the country to keep a list of what they have bought during a three-month period. The department also asks another 7,000 families to keep a daily diary of what they purchase during a two-week period. The Department of Labor then takes these reports and studies the goods and services that are listed. It gives certain items that appear frequently more importance than others that only appear infrequently. The next step is to choose the most important items. It is these most frequently purchased goods and services that are put into the market basket.

The Department of Labor surveys the buying patterns of
7,000 families in major cities to create the market basket,
a representation of the items most often purchased.

Categories of the Market Basket

The market basket items fall into several distinct categories. These categories are as follows, with examples of each:

- **Food and beverages:** Cereals, milk, coffee, chicken, wine, and snacks.

- **Housing:** The money people pay for rent, oil or natural gas to heat the home, and furniture.

The Department of Labor divides its market basket items into several categories, which includes recreational activities such as pets.

- **Clothing:** The clothes men, women, and children wear, as well as jewelry.

- **Transportation:** New and used cars, fares for airlines, mass transit, gasoline, and car insurance.

- **Medical care:** Doctor visits, stays in hospitals, medications, eyeglasses, and other medical services.

- **Recreation:** Television, sports equipment, pets and pet supplies, and things like movie tickets.

- **Education and communication:** College tuition, telephone services, and computer software.

- **Other goods and services:** Cigarettes, haircuts, funeral expenses, and other personal services.

Personal expenses, such as haircuts and coloring, are also considered by the Department of Labor for their market basket.

The Department of Labor includes additional items, such as taxes people pay when they buy certain goods and services and money spent on things like water and sewage bills. Items that are not included are taxes on people's wages (income tax) or money that people spend on investments (like stocks and bonds), real estate (land and houses or apartments), or life insurance.

Data Analysis

The Department of Labor has workers who either visit or call thousands of stores, manufacturers, service providers (such as doctors' and dentists' offices), and other places of business to collect as much information about goods and services as they can. They gather information about the prices being charged as well as how many products are selling. These workers, called economic assistants, record the prices of about 80,000 different items each month. They not only collect the prices of items, but they also register the sizes of cans and bottles that contain some of the products being sold. The reason they do this is so the price recorded is as accurate as possible.

For example, an economic assistant named Marissa noticed that a can of soda cost $1.50 last year and that the same soda still costs $1.50 this year. However, Marissa thought the can of soda looked different. So she checked the amount of soda in the can and discovered that the company that made the soda had changed the size of the can. The can last year held eight ounces. But this year, the can holds only six ounces. So, even though the price is still $1.50, the consumer is buying less soda. If you pay the same amount of money for a smaller can, you are actually paying more because the same amount of money buys you less soda.

Although the prices of common items like soda or pop have seemed to remain unchanged, some companies decreased the size of the packaging. Consumers are actually paying more.

Another Index

The consumer price index (CPI) is just one way to measure inflation. The CPI measures inflation from the point of view of consumers, the people who buy things. There is another index called the producer price index (PPI). The PPI measures inflation from the point of view of the people who make the products. Inflation is also measured by the employment cost index (ECI), which measures inflation from the point of view of the labor market (the workers). The Department of Labor uses its Bureau of Labor Statistics' International Price Program to measure inflation by studying the products that the United States imports (buys from other countries) and exports (products made in the United States and sent to other countries). There is also a study called the Gross Domestic Product Deflator, which measures inflation both by what consumers buy as well as what the government spends.

Another detail that economic assistants look for is a change in value. Let's say that last year a dozen eggs cost $1.45. This year, a dozen eggs cost $2.50. Does this mean that the price is inflated? Or has something in addition to price changed? This time, the economic assistant reads the label on the egg carton. She finds that the same company that sold a dozen eggs last year for $1.45 has switched from selling regular eggs to selling certified organic eggs. To sell certified organic eggs, the egg farmer has to put more money into his chickens, by feeding them better food and providing them with more space, for instance. The customer who buys the certified organic eggs is getting a better product than if he or she bought regular eggs. When a consumer gets better quality (healthier eggs in this case), he or she expects to pay more money. So, the rise in the price of eggs was not caused by inflation.

All of the information that economic assistants collect is sent back to the Department of Labor. There, specialists in economics and commodities (commodities are products that people buy) study and analyze it. These specialists make sure that the economic assistants have not made any mistakes. Once all the information has been verified as correct, the consumer price index is created. The prices of the items in the market basket are compared to similar market basket data from previous years. The specialists compare the baskets from one year to the next to see if overall prices are going up, remaining the same, or going down. It is from this comparison that the specialists decide if the economy is leaning toward inflation, is stagnant (remaining the same), or is experiencing deflation.

Beginning in January 2015, the department now uses a new estimation system. It is designed to improve how the CPI is calculated and offer more flexibility through increased updates and revisions. When it announced the change, the department also said it would no longer use "paper in all steps of producing the CPI." The impact on estimated inflation is yet to be determined, but the change is the department's first major one in 25 years!

CHAPTER 4
Inflation's Effects on the Economy

What are the effects of inflations on the economy and consumers? Are those effects helpful or harmful? People generally speak about inflation in negative terms. Economists, on the other hand, are more generous in their view of inflation. Indeed, economists generally agree that whether inflation impacts us positively or negatively will depend on a number of factors. Let's look at those.

Keeping Inflation Low

The first circumstance to look at is the rate of inflation. Normally, if inflation is between 2 and 3 percent, economists tend to agree that this is a good thing. An inflation rate at this level demonstrates that the economy is growing. Businesses are making profits because most people can afford to buy goods and services. These profits are then put back into the businesses so they can create new products, which grab the attention of even more consumers. Businesses might even offer their employees better wages. This makes their employees happy and also encourages their workers to go out and purchase new goods and services, too. So, you can see how an inflation rate of 2 or 3 percent can help a growing economy grow even healthier.

Let's visit Ian and his lemonade stand again. One day, Ian decided to raise the cost of his lemonade from $1 a glass to $1.03 (a 3 percent increase). Not many people would complain about this inflated price. Another three cents is fairly easy to adjust to. Over the course of the summer, this extra three cents per glass gave Ian an additional $6 profit from the two lemonade stands that he operated.

The next summer, Ian bought three pints of raspberries with his $6 profit from the previous year. Then, he advertised that he had a new product. His customers could buy his regular lemonade for $1.03, as usual. But his new product, raspberry lemonade, would cost them $1.25 per glass. Not everyone wanted to pay extra for the raspberry lemonade, though the new product sounded delicious. But some people did try the raspberry lemonade and loved it. Ian loved it, too. Whereas the regular lemonade gave him a $6 profit at the end of the summer, the raspberry lemonade was popular enough that it also provided him with an additional $6 profit, despite being more expensive to make.

Under these conditions, Ian obviously benefited from the inflation of his prices. He was able to improve the variety of his drinks, and he could give his cousin (who worked the second lemonade stand) an extra $2 for helping him. Ian's customers also benefited. They were able to enjoy Ian's original lemonade with only a three-cent increase. The extra money that they paid inspired Ian to invest in raspberries and create a new drink, one that was enjoyed by a large number of his old customers and that attracted some new customers.

$mart Selling

Like Ian, many kids still use lemonade stands to raise money for themselves or others. If you have similar dreams of making some extra cash, you can do it! Today's Internet environment, however, offers electronic means of making money as a teenager with a flair for business. Popular digital marketplaces include eBay and Etsy. One difference between the two is that Etsy is especially appealing for people who make their own items and consumers who prefer

Popular digital marketplaces like Etsy and eBay make it easier than ever for inspired teens to get a start selling handmade or other products online.

handmade products. The cool thing about both is that they reach consumers worldwide and offer thousands of products. Each has rules that you should study before you make a commitment. Every wise businessperson gets advice from people in their field or from others who can make sure they are not taken advantage of. Consider doing the same.

When inflation rates soar to 10 percent, prices on high-demand items like gasoline begin to rise, too. People such as those on a fixed income struggle to pay.

Harmful Impact of High Inflation

A 3 percent inflation rate is considered a sign of economic health. But if inflation goes higher than 3 percent, a wide range of people may begin to suffer. A 10 percent inflation rate, for instance, would raise the price of Ian's original lemonade to $1.13 per glass. Some people could afford this inflated price because the money they make might have also increased. But the 10 percent hike in price might be too high for other people. Some people, like the retired and elderly, live on a fixed income. That means they receive the same amount of money each year, without any raises. Their income does not keep up with the inflation rate, so what they can spend each year decreases as prices increase.

Here's an example of how a 10 percent inflation rate might hurt someone. Curtis receives an allowance of $10 a week. He has received this same amount ever since he turned twelve years old. Curtis is now fourteen. In the past two years, inflation has increased the prices of most of the things he likes to buy by 10 percent. Since his allowance has not increased at all, Curtis's $10 is actually worth only $8 now. He can buy only $8 worth of goods with his weekly allowance because the 10 percent inflation has deflated the real worth of his allowance. So, when Curtis walks by Ian's lemonade stand, he has to think twice about buying a glass of the juice. He wants to buy a new baseball cap, so he is a little worried about whether he will have enough money for both the cap and the lemonade. The baseball cap he wants cost $8 last year. With the 10 percent inflation, that would increase the price to $8.80 without taxes. Curtis decides not to buy the lemonade.

If there are a lot of people living on fixed incomes, like Curtis, Ian will have fewer customers coming to his stand once prices start to rise. If

When customers are on a fixed income, they have to be more
thoughtful about their purchases. They might put off treats
like lemonade if they have to pay more for necessities.

fewer people buy Ian's lemonade, he might have to lower his prices so that people will be more willing to purchase it. If Ian has to lower his price, he will not make enough profit to give his cousin the extra $2 that he gave him the previous year. Also, Ian will not have enough profit to buy the raspberries and will have to stop offering his popular and profitable raspberry lemonade special.

Inflation and Personal Money Matters

Many parents put money into a savings account for their children's future college costs. Most parents even make adjustments for an inflated cost of college tuition in the future. For instance, the Moores have a ten-year-old daughter. They know that in eight years, their daughter may want to go to the University of Colorado. In 2008, the cost of classes alone (no dorm room, books, or food included in this cost) was about $16,000 a year, or $64,000 for the entire four years of college. The Moores anticipate a normal, relatively low annual increase in the inflation rate (a little more than 4 percent annually), so they are preparing to save $22,000 for each year of their daughter's college, which equals $88,000 for the four years.

What if inflation, over the next eight years, is higher than 4 percent? What if inflation is 5 percent or 10 percent during one or two years of that eight-year period? When it comes time to go to school, the Moores' daughter will have a big decision to make. She will not have enough money to cover all four years of college. She might have to take out loans or get a job at the same time she is going to school. If the inflation rate was really high, she might not be able to attend that school at all.

When it comes time to figure out how much to save for college, students and their families have to take inflation into consideration. Tuition costs might rise in the future.

Calculating Inflation

To hone your understanding of inflation, try using an online inflation calculator. An inflation calculator is a fun way to learn more about the topic of inflation and its effects. There are different ones online, but each provides an eye-opening look into

When you're figuring out your future finances, it's important to factor in inflation. Online calculators can help you see how prices may change in the future.

how price changes during inflation. You can plug in an item, selecting a year for which you'd like to see how much it cost in the past. Price projections are also available when you choose a day in the future. Check price fluctuations over different years for a more complete picture of how prices have changed.

When high inflation hits the economy, the money that people have been saving is no longer worth as much as they had hoped. The money they have saved buys fewer goods and services. During periods of high inflation, people tend to stop buying things like new cars, computers, televisions, houses, and furniture. They usually stop going out to eat in restaurants. They cannot afford to go on vacation or travel to their grandmother's house for Thanksgiving. They stop using the money they have for any extra treats or splurges. They must save their money so they can afford the things that are necessary, such as food, clothing, and home heating. When people stop making purchases, stores suffer financially, as do the businesses that make the goods or offer the services. If inflation is too high, businesses might be forced to cut jobs or even shut down and close up shop completely.

So, inflation can be both helpful and harmful. These are just some ways that inflation affects people's lives and businesses. Although low inflation can be beneficial to a country's economy, high inflation can hurt almost everyone. Trying to keep inflation under control is a complicated job, as will be seen in the next chapter. The task is further complicated by the fact that inflationary forces are complex. They can't all be controlled by a government department, no matter how powerful. A vast multitude of factors and trends—large and small, major and minor—determine the upward or downward movement of the economy. The government has only a few blunt tools with which to service the incredibly complex and delicate machine that is the national and global economy.

Myths and Facts

Myth: All inflation is bad.

Fact: Not all inflation is bad. Inflation can stimulate the economy. Inflation sometimes provides extra money for companies, as well as for their employees. When companies have extra money, they can share their profits with their workers. They can also use that money to develop better products.

Myth: When an economy is experiencing inflation, it means prices for all goods and services are rising.

Fact: This is not necessarily true. Inflation might mean that some products and services have increased in price, while prices for other products and services remain the same or even decrease. Also, some prices for products and services might be rising, but the products and services might have new value-added features (like Blu-ray players in new cars or a new window-washing service added to a standard housecleaning job) that account for at least some of the price increase. A period of inflation features price increases for a large number of—but not necessarily all— popular goods and services over an extended period of time.

Myth: Higher inflation means higher wages.

Fact: Just because the economy is experiencing inflation does not mean that workers will receive higher wages to keep up with that inflation. Sometimes, company owners can't afford to increase the wages of their workers, even if inflation has helped the company owners to earn bigger profits. During an inflationary period, company owners often have to pay higher prices for the materials and services that they have to buy to keep their companies in business. This leaves them with less money with which to offer raises to their employees.

CHAPTER 5

Efforts to Control Inflation

Explaining inflation sometimes takes creativity. A banking museum in England ramped up creativity with its 2008 computer-simulated models involving balloons. Basically, the balloon's air volume depicted inflation or deflation as it expanded or contracted. Visitors used a simulator to control the air, thus keeping the balloon on a steady course.

The simulation was an effective tool in demonstrating how banking officials control inflation to best benefit an economy. A key control mechanism is using interest rates to control inflation.

Interest Rates as a Control Mechanism

In the United States, the Federal Reserve determines the interest rates that banks use. The Federal Reserve, under the direction of the US Congress, regulates (sets the rules for) many of the banks in the country. One of the major roles of the Federal Reserve is to decide which interest rates banks can charge when they offer loans. As seen earlier, the interest rate is the profit that a bank makes when someone borrows money.

When inflation is high, one of the usual causes is that there is too much money circulating in the marketplace. During inflationary periods, people

Federal Reserve Chairman Janet Yellen. The Federal Reserve is
responsible for setting the interest rates used by banks.

have a lot of money and the demand for goods and services is very high, though the supply is low. When 100 people want to buy one glass of lemonade, in other words, Ian could probably ask $20 for the glass and receive it because so many people want that glass of lemonade.

Often, the reason there is a lot of money circulating in the market is because interest rates that banks charge are very low. When interest rates are low, people are encouraged to borrow money to buy things that they want. If you wanted to buy a computer game that cost $50 and all you had was $20, you might make a deal with a friend to borrow the extra $30 that you need. You might tell your friend that instead of just paying her back the $30, you will pay back $31. In this way, your friend can make $1 without doing anything, except lending you the money. So, she might agree to the deal. The one extra dollar that you have to pay her will not be that difficult for you. So, you go buy the computer game, and in a month, you pay back the $31. When bank interest rates are low, it is a good time for people to buy big-ticket items, like houses or cars. This is because they can borrow money from the bank at a low rate. When a lot of people are looking for houses to buy and not that many houses are for sale, then the price of houses rises, or become inflated.

When the Federal Reserve sees that inflation is rising, it raises interest rates. Where interest rates for borrowing money might have been at 5 percent a year, the Federal Reserve might raise the rate to 7 percent. Whereas a lot of people might have been able to afford a loan at 5 percent, when the interest rates reach 7 percent or more, fewer people can afford to take out a loan. This is because it will be more expensive to pay back that loan. A $100,000 loan with a 5 percent annual interest rate would cost $125,000 to pay back in five years, while a 7 percent interest rate would boost that total to $135,000,

Before you make a purchase using a credit card, remember that
interest rates can add considerably to your total cost.

$10,000 more than the loan at 5 percent interest. When interest rates rise, therefore, the demand for loans, as well as the demand for new houses, begins to decrease. When the demand decreases, prices fall, as does inflation.

Using credit cards is similar to taking out a bank loan. Interest rates on a credit card also rise and fall. When the rates are low, people use credit cards to buy new washing machines, televisions, Blu-ray players, and other expensive items. Some people use credit cards to pay for airline tickets and hotels when they go on vacations. However, when interest rates are high, consumers might find that it is very difficult to pay off their credit card debt.

When consumers see how much they have to pay to get out from under their credit card debt, they would be wise to stop buying goods and services until their debt is paid off. If a lot of people are in debt, and they use their money to pay off their bills instead of buying new products, then the demand for goods and services diminishes. And as you know by now, that means prices should begin to fall and inflationary pressures will decrease. If prices and spending levels fall too low, the Federal Reserve may lower interest rates to encourage borrowing and spending and kick-start the slowing economy. These lower rates would make it easier to obtain money, as well as easier to pay down debt at lower interest.

Wages and Inflation

Inflation is not felt as deeply when workers' wages keep up with the inflation rate. So when workers notice that the paychecks they bring home are no longer enough to pay for their house, food, and clothing, they might go to their bosses and ask for more money. When salaries keep up with inflation, when they get higher as inflation gets higher, then increases in

If workers' paychecks do not increase at the same rate as inflation,
it becomes increasingly difficult to make ends meet.

wages help to control inflation. Although inflation continues to rise, so, too, do workers' salaries, so no financial pain is felt.

Stimulating the Economy

If inflation is controlled, it can stimulate the economy and provide profits for businesses and raises in wages for workers. However, if inflation is not controlled, it can send prices so high that buying a loaf of bread can be as dramatic an event as buying a car is now.

Keeping inflation at a reasonable rate is partially the responsibility of the Federal Reserve, which sets the interest rates for banks. Yet, it is individual Americans, in their role as consumers, who perhaps have an even more

Happy Holidays?

Yes, inflation affects our everyday choices as well as how much money we spend throughout the year during holidays. Higher food prices may mean one less protein on your Memorial Day table, or fewer fruits and fresh vegetables for Independence Day. By year's end if inflation is continuing, your family may opt out of its usual bounty of entrees, sides, and desserts and focus on a menu that is more affordable. Year-end gift giving also may be trimmed as your family focuses on having money for a new year. Choosing to curtail holiday spending is a smart response to inflation. It means your family will have money left over for everyday needs.

crucial role in influencing the heating up or cooling down of the economy. When inflation gets too high, people stop buying goods and services that they do not really need. As the demand for goods and services drops, prices usually also drop.

In the end, inflation has its benefits and its dangers. But it is certainly here to stay. Navigating the upward swells of inflation and the sudden plummets of deflation, riding the big waves of a swelling and crashing economy, can be a scary thrill ride. It requires a calm mind, a cool head, and careful planning. If you are smart with your money by, for example, always saving a part of your paycheck in a fund to be used only in times of economic emergency, you will have a sense of security and the reassuring knowledge that you can ride out whatever economic rough waters have been stirred up. You do not have to be a helpless victim of the economy's ups and downs. Instead, you can manage and spend your money wisely, invest it prudently, and save it carefully. You can protect yourself from the uncertainty and panic that often grips the markets and focus instead on calmly enjoying your security and planning for the future and the kind of life you would like to create for yourself.

Ten Great Questions to Ask an Economist

1 How much will college cost when I am old enough to attend?

2 If inflation continues at the same rate as today, what kinds of salaries can I expect to earn in different jobs in the future?

3 What is the rate of inflation today? What was the rate of inflation when my grandparents were my age?

4 I have a small amount of money to invest to eventually help pay for college. Given the current rate of inflation and the economy, and considering likely future trends, where is the best place to put this money? What option would offer the best return on my investment? Which is the safest option, the one that would prevent a loss on my investment?

5 What is happening in the economy today? Are we experiencing inflation or deflation?

6 When the U. S. economy is experiencing inflation, are all the other countries in the world also experiencing inflation?

7 Which is better for an economy, inflation or deflation?

8 When the economy is experiencing an inflation that continues to increase, is it a good idea to buy things now when the prices are lower even if we can't afford them?

9 I have some money saved in the bank. But the interest I earn is only 2 percent. If the inflation rate is at 3 percent, aren't I losing money?

10 My parents told me that because of inflation, our house is worth more today than it was ten years ago when they bought it. But our three-year-old car is worth less. Why is this?

Inflation edges up

*Monthly percentage change in core consumer prices,
which do not include food and energy costs:*

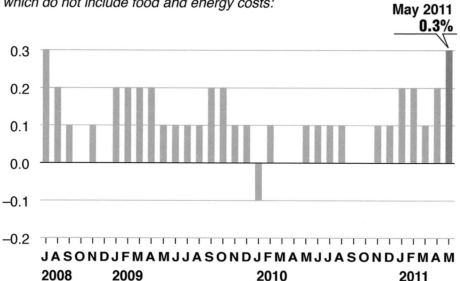

May 2011
0.3%

0.3
0.2
0.1
0.0
−0.1
−0.2

J A S O N D J F M A M J J A S O N D J F M A M J J A S O N D J F M A M

2008   **2009**   **2010**   **2011**

Source: U.S. Bureau of Labor Statistics
Graphic: Scott J. Wilson, Lorraine Wang, Los Angeles Times

© 2011 MCT

As this graph shows, inflation rates can vary wildly over the years.

CHAPTER 6

Inflation Today

For more than three years, the US inflation rate has been lower than the percentage economists generally consider healthy. A 3 percent inflation rate is considered good for the economy. The last time the US rate hit that target was 2011. Instead, it has steadily declined. Generally, the US has experienced zero inflation! As of June 2014, inflation stood at zero (0.8) percent. As of mid-2015, the rate remained flat, dropping a bit lower than the year before to 0.1 percent.

While zero inflation sounds good, remember it's sharply lower than the percentage deemed good for businesses and consumers. The 3 percent target rate provides healthy profits for businesses, while allowing for salary increases to keep up with cost of living hikes. Zero inflation, therefore, is a cause for concern. Eventually steps will be taken to push the rate to a more desirable level. For instance, the Federal Reserve hinted for months in 2015 that it would increase one of its key interest rates. News of that expected increase met with mixed reviews. Yet, the Fed was on target to lift the rate early in 2016.

A Push for Higher Wages

What else has been happening in the economy that affects inflation and may indicate a rise in prices in the United States in the future? One interesting development is a push to raise workers' salaries. The cost of living

A living wage refers to how much money an adult must bring home to support a family. Unfortunately, the federal minimum wage is not enough for families to live on.

in the United States differs between states and cities. So, if your family moved from a small town to a metropolitan area like New York City, your family's earnings would not stretch as far for food, clothing, shelter, and other needs. But, if you move from New York City to a small town, your family's ability to pay for those things would be much greater—even without a raise in pay.

In economics terms, a "living wage" is the amount an adult needs to support his or her family in a specific area. It is generally believed that the minimum wage is simply too low. The federal minimum wage is $7.25 per hour, although some states and cities pay workers more. Across the country, efforts are underway to increase the minimum wage—especially for fast food workers—because it is believed that a $7.25 hourly wage is just not enough money for families to live on. Some propose a goal of $15. Seattle's new law, for example, calls for a $15 minimum wage by 2020, by slowly increasing the hourly rate over the next few years. Meanwhile, on the federal level, President Obama's executive order of 2014 raised the minimum wage to $10.10 for workers on federal construction and service contracts. In July 2015, a bill was introduced in Congress to raise the national minimum to $15.

There is much support and opposition to raising the minimum wage. Some business owners, for example, argue that a higher minimum wage would mean companies will begin cutting their workforces because they

Some feel a higher minimum wage will benefit workers, but others argue that such a salary increase will mean that businesses will have to cut their workforces or close.

cannot to increase salaries to such levels. Others argue that without those increases, workers will continue struggling to meet basic needs.

A Good Move?

People move from one city or state for many reasons. Recent college graduates may move away from home to start a new job. For other workers, a company's relocation to a new area may mean moving to keep work. Other times people leave to find more affordable housing. Sometimes it is to move closer to relatives.

Before moving it is important to get an idea of how much money it will take to live comfortably in an area. It is easier to find such information in today's digital environment. One handy tool is a living wage calculator, like *http://livingwage.mit .edu*. Use it to find out the living wage in a city, costs of common expenses, annual salaries and other information.

Better Job Outlook?

The unemployment rate affects inflation, too. During the recent recession, the economy lost 8.7 million jobs. It has since recovered those. The fact that the rate has improved, however, has not pushed consumer confidence up by a similar hike. Rather, some reports show that consumer confidence still lags as consumers wrestle with issues from the recession and worries about the future.

When the housing market has more buyers than houses,
people bid more than a house's worth. People who saved up
might not be able to afford the house they hoped for.

Worth the Price?

Home sales—another factor that impacts our inflation rate—has rebounded from the recession to the point that home prices are at record highs. Related to this is the shortage of homes for sales in some markets. Two things are happening as a result. First, homes are selling faster than they have in recent years, with many homes only on the market for a couple months. Second, bidding wars are causing homes to be sold and bought at prices higher than the original sales prices.

Can you imagine paying *more* than the cost of a cell phone just because demand is greater than the supply? That might not be a fair or equal analogy to what is happening in the housing market, but it is causing anxiety for people who had saved for homes and now cannot afford to outbid other consumers.

Other Indicators

One other economic indicator that is worth exploring is retail sales. Remember, the retail market slammed during the recession, and afterward. Today, retail sales are substantially better than years ago. Nonetheless, because of stagnant consumer confidence retail sales have been sluggish. In some cases, even popular brands have not done well. Sales of the Apple Watch, for example, fell short of expectation.

Gasoline prices have dropped substantially since the post-recession prices. Gas prices fluctuate, but the price slipped so low that by summer 2015 many drivers paid the lowest price for gas in years. Lower gasoline prices mean more workers can opt to commute by car to work, while families can enjoy more traveling.

In 2015, following the most recent recession, gasoline prices dropped, so families had more money to travel to more places on vacation.

What's Ahead?

What does this all mean? Basically, enjoy zero inflation while it lasts. While economists are not predicting when it will end, inevitably it must. Pushing it toward the preferred 3 percent range will ensure a healthy, more robust economy. It will also mean prices of certain goods and services will increase. Using the strategies in chapter five will enable you to face any increase with calm and wisdom. Learning to do so will position you for future effects of inflation—or deflation. That, in turn, will reveal just how much you understand what inflation is, what it does, and how to be a smart consumer in such economic conditions.

Inflation Timeline

1816 England begins using the gold standard to stop inflation.

1879 US begins using the gold standard.

1884 Bureau of Labor Statistics is created.

1900 US passes the Gold Standard Act.

1913 The Bureau of Labor Statistics begins using the consumer price index.

1913 The Federal Reserve system is created.

November 16, 1914 All Federal Reserve banks open.

1929 The "Great Depression" occurs and people hoard gold.

1965–1982 The "Great Inflation" period.

1973 The Federal Reserve uses policy measures in response to inflation rate increases.

1973 The United States ends use of gold standard.

1979 The inflation rate averages 9 percent.

Paul Voelker becomes the Federal Reserve System chairman and later announces measures to curb inflation.

1980 The inflation rate exceeds 14 percent.

President Jimmy Carter signs the Monetary Control Act of 1980 into law.

1980–1982 The United States experiences another recession.

Late 1980s Inflation rate averages 3.5 percent.

Late 1980s–Early 1990s During the banking crises many savings and loan banks close.

1982–2007 During this "Great Moderation" period, inflation is low and stable.

December 2007–June 2009 During the "Great Recession," inflation rates do not fall as much as anticipated.

October 2009 Inflation rate drops below zero, representing negative inflation.

January 2015 The Bureau of Labor Statistics begins using a new system for estimating Consumer Price Index.

March 2015 Inflation rate drops below zero for first time since 2009.

Bibliographic Sources

Ball, R.J. *Inflation and the Theory of Money.* Piscataway, NJ: Aldine Transaction, 2007.

Bank of England Museum. "The Pound in Your Pocket Exhibition." Retrieved September 2008 (*http://www. bankofengland.co.uk/education/ museum/exhibitions/current.htm*).

Bureau of Labor Statistics. "BLS History/Timeline." US Department of Labor. Retrieved July 22, 2015 (*http://www.bls.gov/bls/history/ timeline.htm*).

Bureau of Labor Statistics. "Inflation and Prices." US Department of Labor. Retrieved October 22, 2015 (*http://www.bls.gov/data/*).

Bureau of Labor Statistics. "New CPI Estimation System To Be Introduced." US Department of Labor. Retrieved July 22, 2015 (*http:// www.bls.gov/cpi/cpinewest.htm*).

Davies, Glyn, and Roy Davies. *A History of Money From Ancient Times to the Present Day.* Cardiff, Wales: University of Wales Press, 2002.

Federal Reserve Bank of Richmond. "Events Timeline." Retrieved July 22, 2015 (*http://www.federalreservehistory.org/Events/ GraphicalView/13*).

Ferguson, Niall. *The Ascent of Money: A Financial History of the World.* New York, NY: Penguin Press, 2008.

Hanes, Chris. "Prices and Price Indices." *Historical Statistics of the United States.* Edited by Susan B. Carter, Scott S. Gartner, Michael Haines, Alan L. Olmstead, Richard Sutch, and Gavin Wright. New York, NY: Cambridge University Press, 2002.

InflationData.com. "Food Price Inflation." Retrieved July 22, 2015 (*http://inflationdata.com/articles/2013/03/21/food-price-inflation-1913*).

Klein, Grady and Yoram Bauman. *The Cartoon Introduction to Economics. Volume One: Microeconomics.* New York, NY: Hill and Wang, 2010.

McGreal, Chris. "What Comes After a Trillion: Inflation in Zimbabwe." *The Guardian,* July 18, 2008, p. 12.

Mishkin, Frederic S. *Monetary Policy Strategy.* Cambridge, MA: MIT Press, 2007.

Nova. "The History of Money." PBS.org, August 2002. Retrieved October 22, 2015 (*http://www.pbs.org/wgbh/nova/moolah/history.html*).

Patton, Mike. "Consumer Price Index Undergoes Most Significant Change in 25 Years." Retrieved July 22, 2015 (*http://www.forbes.com/sites/mikepatton/2015/01/29/consumer-price-index-undergoes-most-significant-change-in-25-years/*).

Salvatore, Dominick, and Eugene Diulio. *Principles of Economics.* New York, NY: McGraw Hill, 2008.

Samuelson, Robert J. *The Great Inflation and Its Aftermath: The Past and Future of American Affluence.* New York, NY: Random House, 2008.

Swaneberg, August. *Macroeconomics Demystified.* New York, NY: McGraw-Hill, 2005.

Voda, David. *Inflation-Proof Your Portfolio: How to Protect Your Money From the Coming Government Hyperinflation.* Hoboken, NJ: Wiley & Sons, 2012.

Glossary

barter—To trade goods or services without the exchange of money.

commodity—An article of trade or commerce, especially an agricultural or mining product that can be processed and resold.

consumer price index (CPI)—A measurement of the prices of goods and services bought by consumers. It is used to gauge inflation.

cost-push inflation—Persistent increase in prices that results from higher production costs that are then reflected in the price of products.

currency—Money in any form that is used as a medium of exchange, especially circulating paper money.

deflation—A persistent decrease in the level of consumer prices.

demand-pull inflation—Persistent increase in prices that results from an increase in the demand for goods and services by households, the government, businesses, or foreign countries.

devalue—To lessen the value of something; to lower the exchange value.

economics—The study of the economy.

economy—A careful management of resources, such as money, and the system of economic activity in a country.

Federal Reserve—The central controlling bank of the United States that sets the laws by which all other US banks function.

fixed income—Revenue that remains constant, regardless of changing economic factors such as inflation.

goods and services—Things that people buy. Goods, like television sets or cars, are tangible objects that are purchased and used by the consumer. Services, like haircuts or house cleaning, are things that are done for you when you pay for them.

hyperinflation—Extremely high inflation or inflation that is out of control.

inflation—A general increase in the prices of goods and services over a period of time.

interest rate—The rate that a bank charges when a person takes out a loan.

market basket—A group of almost 80,000 popular goods and services used to calculate the consumer price index.

profits—The money that a business makes after all the bills are paid.

purchasing (or buying) power—The amount of goods and services that a dollar can buy.

reinvest—To put money back into a business or an investment commodity.

Further Reading

Books

Conaghan, Daniel. *The Book Of Money: Everything You Need To Know About How Finances Work.* Buffalo, NY: Firefly Books, 2013.

Klein, Grady and Yoram Bauman. *The Cartoon Introduction to Economics. Volume One: Microeconomics.* New York: Hill and Wang. 2010.

Meyer, Terry Teague. *How Inflation Affects You.* New York, NY: Rosen Publishing Group, 2013.

Tyson, Eric. *Personal Finance For Dummies.* Hoboken, NJ: John Wiley & Sons, Inc. 2012.

Websites

Bureau of Labor Statistics
www.bls.gov/k2/students.htm
Videos, activities, career exploration, and other resources.

Bureau of Labor Statistics
www.bls.gov/CPI/
Information about the consumer price index.

InflationData.com
inflationdata.com
Articles, blog, calculators, and other inflation-related resources.

Investopedia's Inflation Page
www.investopedia.com/terms/i/inflation.asp
Discussion of inflation with easy-to-understand video.

The ConsumerMan Show: Managing Your Money
www.youtube.com/watch?v=BkQot37m-4c&list=PL5C570F858BAEE1F7&
index=2
Video about money management topics.

The Library of Economics and Liberty
www.econlib.org/library/Enc/Inflation.html
Resource for understanding inflation.

Index